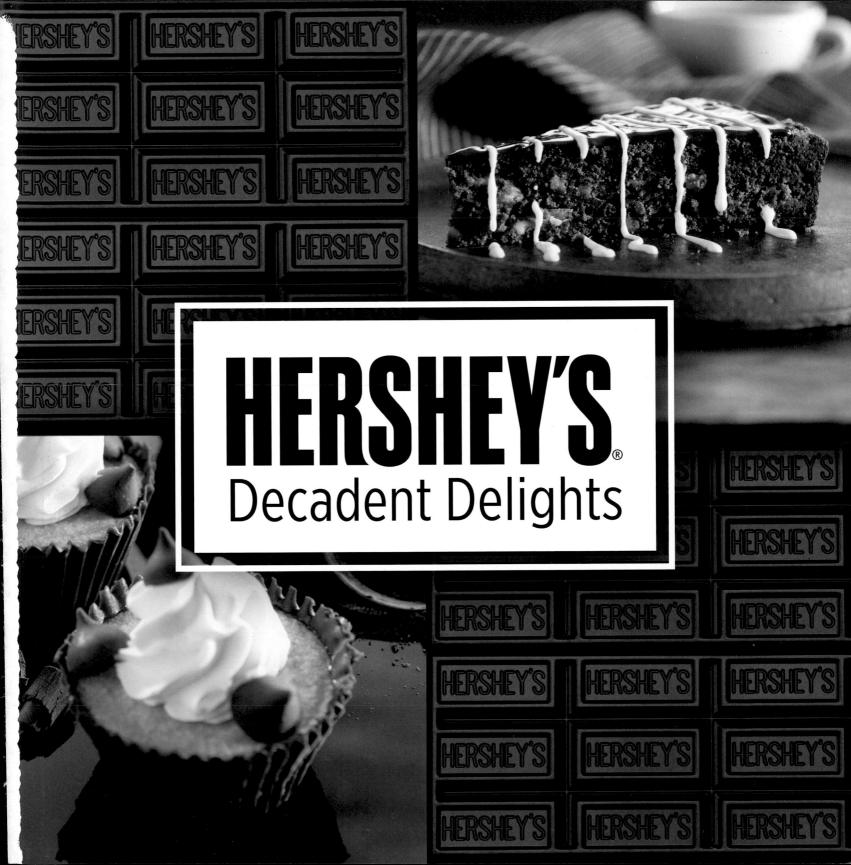

HERSHEY'S®
Decadent Delights

Pictured on the front cover *(top to bottom)*: HERSHEY'S White and Dark Chocolate Fudge Torte *(page 112)* and MINI KISSES® Pumpkin Mousse Cups *(page 118)*.
Pictured on the back cover *(left to right)*: Chocolate Almond Torte *(page 44)* and White & Chocolate Covered Strawberries *(page 99)*.
Pictured on the inside back flap: Chocolate Almond Macaroon Bars *(page 24)*.

ISBN-13: 978-1-68022-305-7

Manufactured in China.

8 7 6 5 4 3 2 1

Microwave Cooking: Microwave ovens vary in wattage. Use the cooking times as guidelines and check for doneness before adding more time.

TABLE OF CONTENTS

COOKIES & BITES

Secret KISSES® Cookies

1 cup (2 sticks) butter or margarine, softened

½ cup granulated sugar

1 teaspoon vanilla extract

1¾ cups all-purpose flour

1 cup finely chopped walnuts or almonds

36 HERSHEY'S KISSES BRAND Milk Chocolates or HERSHEY'S KISSES BRAND Milk Chocolates with Almonds

Powdered sugar for rolling

1. Beat butter, granulated sugar and vanilla with mixer on medium speed in large bowl until fluffy. Add flour and walnuts; beat on low speed of mixer until well blended. Cover; refrigerate 1 to 2 hours or until dough is firm enough to handle.

2. Remove wrappers from chocolates. Heat oven to 375°F. Using about 1 tablespoon dough for each cookie, shape dough around each chocolate; roll in hand to make ball. (Be sure to cover each chocolate piece completely.) Place on ungreased cookie sheet.

3. Bake 10 to 12 minutes or until cookies are set but not browned. Cool slightly; remove to wire rack. While still slightly warm, roll in powdered sugar. Cool completely. Store in tightly covered container. Roll again in powdered sugar just before serving.

Variation: Sift together 1 tablespoon HERSHEY'S Cocoa with ⅓ cup powdered sugar. Roll warm cookies in cocoa mixture. ◼

Double Chocolate Coconut Oatmeal Cookies

1 cup shortening

1¾ cups packed light brown sugar

3 eggs

2 teaspoons vanilla extract

1⅓ cups all-purpose flour

½ cup HERSHEY'S Cocoa

2 teaspoons baking soda

¼ teaspoon salt

½ cup water

3 cups rolled oats or quick-cooking oats

2 cups (12-ounce package) HERSHEY'S SPECIAL DARK Chocolate Chips or HERSHEY'S Semi-Sweet Chocolate Chips, divided

2 cups MOUNDS Sweetened Coconut Flakes, divided

1 cup coarsely chopped nuts

1. Beat shortening, brown sugar, eggs and vanilla in large bowl until well blended. Stir together flour, cocoa, baking soda and salt; add alternately with water to shortening mixture. Stir in oats, 1 cup chocolate chips, 1 cup coconut and nuts, blending well. Cover; refrigerate 2 hours.

2. Heat oven to 350°F. Lightly grease cookie sheet or line with parchment paper. Using ¼-cup ice cream scoop or measuring cup, drop dough about 4 inches apart onto prepared cookie sheet. Sprinkle cookie tops with remaining coconut. Top with remaining chocolate chips (about 9 chips per cookie); lightly press into dough.

3. Bake 10 to 12 minutes or until set (do not overbake). Cool slightly; remove from cookie sheet to wire rack. Cool completely. ■

Rich Cocoa Crinkle Cookies

2 cups granulated sugar

¾ cup vegetable oil

1 cup HERSHEY'S Cocoa

4 eggs

2 teaspoons vanilla extract

2⅓ cups all-purpose flour

2 teaspoons baking powder

½ teaspoon salt

Powdered sugar for rolling

1. Combine granulated sugar and oil in large bowl; add cocoa, beating until well blended. Beat in eggs and vanilla. Stir together flour, baking powder and salt. Gradually add to cocoa mixture, beating well.

2. Cover; refrigerate until dough is firm enough to handle, at least 6 hours.

3. Heat oven to 350°F. Lightly grease cookie sheet or line with parchment paper. Shape dough into 1-inch balls; roll in powdered sugar to coat. Place about 2 inches apart on prepared cookie sheet.

4. Bake 10 to 12 minutes or until almost no indentation remains when touched lightly and tops are crackled. Cool slightly. Remove from cookie sheet to wire rack. Cool completely. ■

KISSES® Coconut Macaroon Blossoms

⅓ cup butter or margarine, softened

1 package (3 ounces) cream cheese, softened

¾ cup sugar

1 egg yolk

2 teaspoons almond extract

2 teaspoons orange juice

1¼ cups all-purpose flour

2 teaspoons baking powder

¼ teaspoon salt

5 cups MOUNDS Sweetened Coconut Flakes, divided

48 HERSHEY'S KISSESBRAND Milk Chocolates

1. Beat butter, cream cheese and sugar with mixer on medium speed in large bowl until well blended. Add egg yolk, almond extract and orange juice; beat well. Stir together flour, baking powder and salt; gradually add to butter mixture. Stir in 3 cups coconut. Cover; refrigerate 1 hour or until firm enough to handle. Meanwhile, remove wrappers from chocolates.

2. Heat oven to 350°F.

3. Shape dough into 1-inch balls; roll in remaining 2 cups coconut. Place on ungreased cookie sheet.

4. Bake 10 to 12 minutes or until lightly browned. Remove from oven; immediately press chocolate piece into center of each cookie. Cool 1 minute. Carefully remove to wire rack and cool completely. ■

Peanut Butter Cut-Out Cookies

½ cup (1 stick) butter or margarine

1 cup REESE'S Peanut Butter Chips

⅔ cup packed light brown sugar

1 egg

¾ teaspoon vanilla extract

1⅓ cups all-purpose flour

¾ teaspoon baking soda

½ cup finely chopped pecans

CHOCOLATE CHIP GLAZE (recipe follows)

1. Place butter and peanut butter chips in large microwave-safe bowl. Microwave at MEDIUM (50%) 1 minute; stir until chips are melted. Add brown sugar, egg and vanilla, beating until well blended. Stir in flour, baking soda and pecans, blending well. Refrigerate 15 to 20 minutes or until firm enough to roll.

2. Heat oven to 350°F.

3. Roll a small portion of dough at a time on lightly floured board, or between 2 pieces of wax paper, to ¼-inch thickness. (Keep remaining dough in refrigerator.) With cookie cutters, cut dough into desired shapes; place on ungreased cookie sheets.

4. Bake 7 to 8 minutes or until almost set (do not overbake). Cool 1 minute; remove from cookie sheets to wire racks. Cool completely. Drizzle CHOCOLATE CHIP GLAZE onto each cookie; allow to set.

Chocolate Chip Glaze:
Place 1 cup HERSHEY'S SPECIAL DARK Chocolate Chips or HERSHEY'S Semi-Sweet Chocolate Chips and 1 tablespoon shortening (do not use butter, margarine, spread or oil) in small microwave-safe bowl. Microwave at MEDIUM (50%) 1 minute; stir. If necessary, microwave at MEDIUM an additional 15 seconds at a time, stirring after each heating, just until chips are melted and mixture is smooth. ■

KISSES® Peanut Butter Blossoms

MAKES ABOUT 48 COOKIES

48 HERSHEY'S KISSES_{BRAND} Milk Chocolates

¾ cup REESE'S Creamy Peanut Butter

½ cup shortening

⅓ cup granulated sugar

⅓ cup packed light brown sugar

1 egg

2 tablespoons milk

1 teaspoon vanilla extract

1½ cups all-purpose flour

1 teaspoon baking soda

½ teaspoon salt

⅓ cup additional granulated sugar for rolling

1. Heat oven to 375°F. Remove wrappers from chocolates.

2. Beat peanut butter and shortening with mixer on medium speed in large bowl until well blended. Add ⅓ cup granulated sugar and brown sugar; beat until fluffy. Add egg, milk and vanilla; beat well. Stir together flour, baking soda and salt; gradually beat into peanut butter mixture.

3. Shape dough into 1-inch balls. Roll in additional granulated sugar; place on ungreased cookie sheet.

4. Bake 8 to 10 minutes or until lightly browned. Immediately press a chocolate into center of each cookie; cookies will crack around edges. Remove to wire racks and cool completely. ■

Double-Drizzled Chocolate Shortbread Cookies

2 cups (4 sticks) butter or margarine, softened

1⅓ cups sugar

1 teaspoon vanilla extract

4 egg yolks

4 cups all-purpose flour

½ cup HERSHEY'S SPECIAL DARK Cocoa

1 teaspoon salt

1 cup chopped pecans

1 cup HERSHEY'S SPECIAL DARK Chocolate Chips or HERSHEY'S Semi-Sweet Chocolate Chips

2 tablespoons shortening (do not use butter, margarine, spread or oil), divided

1 cup REESE'S Peanut Butter Chips or HERSHEY'S Premier White Chips

1. Beat butter, sugar and vanilla until well blended. Add egg yolks, one at a time, beating well after each addition. Gradually add flour, cocoa and salt, beating until blended. (Batter is very stiff.)

2. Divide dough in half. Shape each part into 12-inch-long log. Roll each in pecans, pressing firmly to have pecans adhere. Wrap each roll separately in plastic wrap. Refrigerate 6 to 8 hours.

3. Heat oven to 350°F. Using a sharp knife, cut rolls into ⅜-inch slices. Place on ungreased cookie sheet. Bake 10 to 12 minutes or until set. Cool slightly. Remove from cookie sheet to wire rack. Cool completely.

4. Place chocolate chips and 1 tablespoon shortening in small microwave-safe bowl. Microwave at MEDIUM (50%) 1 minute; stir. If necessary, microwave at MEDIUM an additional 15 seconds at a time, stirring after each heating, until chips are melted and smooth when stirred. Drizzle over tops of cookies. Melt peanut butter chips or white chips with remaining 1 tablespoon shortening; drizzle over chocolate. Let stand until drizzles are set. ■

HERSHEY'S® MINI KISSES® Milk Chocolate Peanut Butter Cookies

¼ cup (½ stick) butter or margarine, softened

¼ cup REESE'S Creamy Peanut Butter

¼ cup granulated sugar

¼ cup packed light brown sugar

1 egg

½ teaspoon vanilla extract

⅔ cup all-purpose flour

¼ teaspoon baking soda

⅛ teaspoon salt

1¾ cups (10-ounce package) HERSHEY'S MINI KISSES BRAND Milk Chocolates

1. Heat oven to 350°F. Lightly grease cookie sheet or line with parchment paper.

2. Beat butter and peanut butter in large bowl on medium speed of mixer until creamy. Gradually add granulated sugar and brown sugar, beating until well mixed. Add egg and vanilla; beat until light and fluffy. Stir together flour, baking soda and salt; add to butter mixture, beating until well blended. Stir in chocolates. Drop batter by rounded tablespoons onto prepared cookie sheet.

3. Bake 10 to 12 minutes or until lightly browned. Cool slightly; remove from cookie sheet to wire rack. Cool completely. ■

Chocolate Seven Layer Bars

1½ cups finely crushed thin pretzels or pretzel sticks

¾ cup (1½ sticks) butter or margarine, melted

1 can (14 ounces) sweetened condensed milk (not evaporated milk)

1 package (4 ounces) HERSHEY'S Unsweetened Chocolate Baking Bar, broken into pieces

2 cups miniature marshmallows

1 cup MOUNDS Sweetened Coconut Flakes

1 cup coarsely chopped pecans

1 package (4 ounces) HERSHEY'S Semi-Sweet Chocolate Baking Bar, broken into pieces

1 tablespoon shortening (do not use butter, margarine, spread or oil)

1. Heat oven to 350°F. Combine pretzels and melted butter in small bowl; press evenly onto bottom of ungreased 13×9×2-inch baking pan.

2. Place sweetened condensed milk and unsweetened chocolate in small microwave-safe bowl. Microwave at MEDIUM (50%) 1 minute; stir. If necessary, microwave at MEDIUM an additional 15 seconds at a time, stirring after each heating, until mixture is melted and smooth when stirred. Carefully pour over pretzel layer in pan. Top with marshmallows, coconut and pecans; press firmly down onto chocolate layer.

3. Bake 25 to 30 minutes or until lightly browned; cool completely in pan on wire rack.

4. Melt semi-sweet chocolate and shortening in small microwave-safe bowl at MEDIUM (50%) 1 minute or until melted when stirred; drizzle over entire top. Refrigerate 15 minutes or until glaze is set. Cut into bars. ■

Best Fudgey Pecan Brownies

½ cup (1 stick) butter or margarine, melted

1 cup sugar

1 teaspoon vanilla extract

2 eggs

½ cup all-purpose flour

⅓ cup HERSHEY'S Cocoa

¼ teaspoon baking powder

¼ teaspoon salt

½ cup coarsely chopped pecans

CHOCOLATE PECAN FROSTING (recipe follows)

Pecan halves

1. Heat oven to 350°F. Lightly grease 8- or 9-inch square baking pan.

2. Beat butter, sugar and vanilla with spoon in large bowl. Add eggs; beat well. Stir together flour, cocoa, baking powder and salt; gradually add to egg mixture, beating until well blended. Stir in chopped pecans. Spread in prepared pan.

3. Bake 20 to 25 minutes or until brownies begin to pull away from sides of pan. Meanwhile, prepare CHOCOLATE PECAN FROSTING. Spread warm frosting over warm brownies. Garnish with pecan halves. Cool completely; cut into squares.

CHOCOLATE PECAN FROSTING

MAKES ABOUT 1 CUP FROSTING

1⅓ cups powdered sugar

2 tablespoons HERSHEY'S Cocoa

3 tablespoons butter or margarine

2 tablespoons milk

¼ teaspoon vanilla extract

¼ cup chopped pecans

1. Stir together powdered sugar and cocoa in medium bowl.

2. Heat butter and milk in small saucepan over low heat until butter is melted. Gradually beat into cocoa mixture, beating until smooth. Stir in vanilla and pecans. ■

Chocolate Almond Macaroon Bars

2 cups chocolate wafer cookie crumbs

6 tablespoons butter or margarine, melted

6 tablespoons powdered sugar

1 can (14 ounces) sweetened condensed milk (not evaporated milk)

3¾ cups MOUNDS Sweetened Coconut Flakes

1 cup sliced almonds, toasted* (optional)

1 cup HERSHEY'S SPECIAL DARK Chocolate Chips or HERSHEY'S Semi-Sweet Chocolate Chips

¼ cup whipping cream

½ cup HERSHEY'S Premier White Chips

*To toast almonds: Heat oven to 350°F. Spread almonds evenly on shallow baking sheet. Bake 5 to 8 minutes or until lightly browned.

1. Heat oven to 350°F. Grease 13×9×2-inch baking pan.

2. Combine crumbs, melted butter and powdered sugar in large bowl. Firmly press crumb mixture on bottom of prepared pan. Stir together sweetened condensed milk, coconut and almonds in large bowl, mixing well. Carefully drop mixture by spoonfuls over crust; spread evenly.

3. Bake 20 to 25 minutes or until coconut edges just begin to brown. Cool.

4. Place chocolate chips and whipping cream in medium microwave-safe bowl. Microwave at MEDIUM (50%) 1 minute; stir. If necessary, microwave at MEDIUM an additional 15 seconds at a time, stirring after each heating, until chips are melted and mixture is smooth when stirred. Cool until slightly thickened; spread over cooled bars. Sprinkle top with white chips. Cover; refrigerate several hours or until thoroughly chilled. Cut into bars. Refrigerate leftovers. ■

Chocolate Orange Cheesecake Bars

1 cup all-purpose flour

½ cup packed light brown sugar

¼ teaspoon ground cinnamon (optional)

⅓ cup shortening

½ cup chopped pecans

CHOCOLATE ORANGE FILLING (recipe follows)

Pecan halves (optional)

1. Heat oven to 350°F.

2. Stir together flour, brown sugar and cinnamon, if desired, in large bowl. Cut shortening into flour mixture with pastry blender or two knives until mixture resembles coarse crumbs. Stir in chopped pecans. Reserve ¾ cup flour mixture. Press remaining mixture firmly onto bottom of ungreased 9-inch square baking pan. Bake 10 minutes or until lightly browned.

3. Spread CHOCOLATE ORANGE FILLING over warm crust. Sprinkle with reserved flour mixture. Press pecan halves lightly onto top, if desired. Return to oven. Bake 25 to 30 minutes or until lightly browned. Cool; cut into bars. Cover; refrigerate leftover bars.

CHOCOLATE ORANGE FILLING

1 package (8 ounces) cream cheese, softened

⅔ cup sugar

⅓ cup HERSHEY'S Cocoa

¼ cup milk

1 egg

1 teaspoon vanilla extract

¼ teaspoon freshly grated orange peel

Beat cream cheese and sugar with electric mixer on medium speed in medium bowl until fluffy. Add cocoa, milk, egg, vanilla and orange peel; beat until smooth. ■

Peanut Butter Fudge Brownie Bars

MAKES ABOUT 24 BARS

1 cup (2 sticks) butter or margarine, melted

1½ cups sugar

2 eggs

1 teaspoon vanilla extract

1¼ cups all-purpose flour

⅔ cup HERSHEY'S Cocoa

¼ cup milk

1¼ cups chopped pecans or walnuts, divided

½ cup (1 stick) butter or margarine

1⅔ cups (10-ounce package) REESE'S Peanut Butter Chips

1 can (14 ounces) sweetened condensed milk (not evaporated milk)

¼ cup HERSHEY'S SPECIAL DARK Chocolate Chips or HERSHEY'S Semi-Sweet Chocolate Chips

1. Heat oven to 350°F. Grease 13×9×2-inch baking pan.

2. Beat melted butter, sugar, eggs and vanilla in large bowl with mixer on medium speed until well blended. Add flour, cocoa and milk; beat until blended. Stir in 1 cup nuts. Spread in prepared pan.

3. Bake 25 to 30 minutes or just until edges begin to pull away from sides of pan. Cool completely in pan on wire rack.

4. Melt ½ cup butter and peanut butter chips in medium saucepan over low heat, stirring constantly. Add sweetened condensed milk, stirring until smooth; pour over baked layer.

5. Place chocolate chips in small microwave-safe bowl. Microwave at MEDIUM (50%) 45 seconds or just until chips are melted when stirred. Drizzle bars with melted chocolate; sprinkle with remaining ¼ cup nuts. Refrigerate 1 hour or until firm. Cut into bars. Cover; refrigerate leftover bars. ■

MINI KISSES® Fruit Bars

1½ cups all-purpose flour

1½ cups quick-cooking rolled oats

1 cup packed light brown sugar

1 teaspoon baking powder

¾ cup (1½ sticks) cold butter or margarine

1 jar (10 to 12 ounces) raspberry jam

1¾ cups (10-ounce package) HERSHEY'S MINI KISSESBRAND Milk Chocolates

½ cup chopped nuts (optional)

1. Heat oven to 350°F. Lightly grease 13×9×2-inch baking pan.

2. Combine flour, oats, brown sugar and baking powder in large bowl. Cut butter into flour mixture with pastry blender or two knives until crumbly. Remove 2 cups crumb mixture; set aside.

3. Press remaining crumb mixture onto bottom of prepared pan. Stir jam to soften; carefully spread over crumb mixture. Sprinkle chocolates evenly over jam. Cover with reserved crumbs. Sprinkle nuts over top, if desired; press firmly.

4. Bake 40 to 45 minutes or until lightly browned. Cool completely in pan on wire rack. Cut into bars. ■

Chocolate Streusel Bars

1¾ cups all-purpose flour

1 cup sugar

¼ cup HERSHEY'S Cocoa

½ cup (1 stick) butter or margarine

1 egg

1 can (14 ounces) sweetened condensed milk (not evaporated milk)

2 cups (12-ounce package) HERSHEY'S SPECIAL DARK Chocolate Chips or HERSHEY'S Semi-Sweet Chocolate Chips, divided

1 cup coarsely chopped nuts

1. Heat oven to 350°F. Grease 13×9×2-inch baking pan.

2. Stir together flour, sugar and cocoa in large bowl. Cut in butter until mixture resembles coarse crumbs. Add egg; mix well. Set aside 1½ cups mixture. Press remaining mixture onto bottom of prepared pan. Bake crust 10 minutes.

3. Meanwhile, place sweetened condensed milk and 1 cup chocolate chips in medium microwave-safe bowl; stir. Microwave at MEDIUM (50%) 1 to 1½ minutes or until chips are melted and mixture is smooth when stirred; pour over crust. Add nuts and remaining chips to reserved crumb mixture. Sprinkle over top.

4. Bake an additional 25 to 30 minutes or until center is almost set. Cool completely in pan on wire rack. Cut into bars. ■

Five Layer Bars

¾ cup (1½ sticks) butter or margarine

1¾ cups graham cracker crumbs

¼ cup HERSHEY'S Cocoa

2 tablespoons sugar

1 can (14 ounces) sweetened condensed milk (not evaporated milk)

1 cup HERSHEY'S SPECIAL DARK Chocolate Chips or HERSHEY'S Semi-Sweet Chocolate Chips

1 cup raisins, chopped dried apricots or miniature marshmallows

1 cup chopped nuts

1. Heat oven to 350°F. Place butter in 13×9×2-inch baking pan. Heat in oven until melted; remove pan from oven.

2. Stir together crumbs, cocoa and sugar; sprinkle evenly over butter. Pour sweetened condensed milk evenly over crumb mixture. Sprinkle with chocolate chips and raisins. Sprinkle nuts on top; press down firmly.

3. Bake 25 to 30 minutes or until lightly browned. Cool completely in pan on wire rack. Cover with foil; let stand at room temperature 6 to 8 hours. Cut into bars.

Golden Bars: Substitute 1 cup REESE'S Peanut Butter Chips for chocolate chips. Sprinkle 1 cup golden raisins or chopped dried apricots over chips. Proceed as above. ■

English Toffee Bars

2 cups all-purpose flour

1 cup packed light brown sugar

½ cup (1 stick) cold butter

1 cup pecan halves

TOFFEE TOPPING (recipe follows)

1 cup HERSHEY'S Milk Chocolate Chips

1. Heat oven to 350°F.

2. Combine flour and brown sugar in large bowl. With pastry blender or fork, cut in butter until fine crumbs form (a few large crumbs may remain). Press mixture onto bottom of ungreased 13×9×2-inch baking pan. Sprinkle pecans over crust. Prepare TOFFEE TOPPING; drizzle evenly over pecans and crust.

3. Bake 20 to 22 minutes or until topping is bubbly and golden; remove from oven. Immediately sprinkle milk chocolate chips evenly over top; press gently onto surface. Cool completely in pan on wire rack. Cut into bars.

Toffee Topping: Combine ⅔ cup butter and ⅓ cup packed light brown sugar in small saucepan; cook over medium heat, stirring constantly, until mixture comes to a boil. Continue boiling, stirring constantly, 30 seconds. Use immediately. ■

European Mocha Fudge Cake

MAKES 12 SERVINGS

1¼ cups (2½ sticks) butter or margarine

¾ cup HERSHEY'S SPECIAL DARK Cocoa

4 eggs

¼ teaspoon salt

1 teaspoon vanilla extract

2 cups sugar

1 cup all-purpose flour

1 cup finely chopped pecans

CREAMY COFFEE FILLING (recipe follows)

Chocolate curls (optional)

1. Heat oven to 350°F. Butter bottom and sides of two 9-inch round baking pans. Line bottoms with wax paper; butter paper.

2. Melt butter in small saucepan; remove from heat. Add cocoa, stirring until blended; cool slightly. Beat eggs in large bowl until foamy; add salt and vanilla. Gradually add sugar, beating well. Add cooled chocolate mixture; blend thoroughly. Fold in flour. Stir in pecans. Pour mixture into prepared pans.

3. Bake 20 to 25 minutes or until wooden pick inserted in center comes out clean. Do not overbake. Cool 5 minutes; remove from pans to wire racks. Carefully peel off paper. Cool completely. Spread CREAMY COFFEE FILLING between layers, over top and sides of cake. Garnish with chocolate curls, if desired. Refrigerate 1 hour or longer before serving. Cover leftover cake; store in refrigerator.

Make Ahead Directions: Cooled cake may be wrapped and frozen up to 4 weeks; thaw, wrapped, before filling and frosting.

CREAMY COFFEE FILLING

MAKES ABOUT 3 CUPS FILLING

1½ cups cold whipping cream

⅓ cup packed light brown sugar

2 teaspoons powdered instant coffee

Combine all ingredients; stir until instant coffee is almost dissolved. Beat until stiff. ■

Chocolate Lemon Marble Cake

2½ cups all-purpose flour

1¾ cups plus ⅓ cup sugar, divided

2 teaspoons baking powder

1¼ teaspoons baking soda, divided

½ teaspoon salt

⅓ cup butter or margarine, softened

⅓ cup shortening

3 eggs

1⅔ cups buttermilk or sour milk*

2 teaspoons vanilla extract

⅓ cup HERSHEY'S Cocoa

¼ cup water

2 teaspoons freshly grated lemon peel

¼ teaspoon lemon juice

COCOA GLAZE (recipe follows)

*To sour milk: Use 1 tablespoon plus 2 teaspoons white vinegar plus milk to equal 1⅔ cups.

1. Heat oven to 375°F. Grease and flour 12-cup fluted tube pan.**

2. Stir together flour, 1¾ cups sugar, baking powder, 1 teaspoon baking soda and salt in large bowl. Add butter, shortening, eggs, buttermilk and vanilla; beat on medium speed of mixer 3 minutes.

3. Stir together cocoa, remaining ⅓ cup sugar, remaining ¼ teaspoon baking soda and water; blend into ⅔ cup vanilla batter. Blend lemon peel and lemon juice into remaining vanilla batter; drop spoonfuls of lemon batter into prepared pan. Drop spoonfuls of chocolate batter on top of lemon batter; swirl with knife or metal spatula for marbled effect.

4. Bake 35 to 40 minutes or until wooden pick inserted in center comes out clean. Cool 15 minutes; remove from pan to wire rack. Cool completely. Glaze with COCOA GLAZE.

**Cake may also be baked in two 9×5×3-inch loaf pans. Bake 40 to 45 minutes or until wooden pick inserted in center comes out clean.

COCOA GLAZE

MAKES ABOUT 1½ CUPS GLAZE

¼ cup HERSHEY'S Cocoa

3 tablespoons light corn syrup

4 teaspoons water

½ teaspoon vanilla extract

1 cup powdered sugar

Combine cocoa, corn syrup and water in small saucepan; cook over medium heat, stirring constantly, until mixture thickens. Remove from heat; blend in vanilla and powdered sugar. Beat until smooth. ∎

HERSHEY'S® "Perfectly Chocolate" Chocolate Cake

2 cups sugar

1¾ cups all-purpose flour

¾ cup HERSHEY'S Cocoa

1½ teaspoons baking powder

1½ teaspoons baking soda

1 teaspoon salt

2 eggs

1 cup milk

½ cup vegetable oil

2 teaspoons vanilla extract

1 cup boiling water

"PERFECTLY CHOCOLATE" CHOCOLATE FROSTING (recipe follows)

1. Heat oven to 350°F. Grease and flour two 9-inch round baking pans.

2. Stir together sugar, flour, cocoa, baking powder, baking soda and salt in large bowl. Add eggs, milk, oil and vanilla; beat on medium speed of mixer 2 minutes. Stir in boiling water (batter will be thin). Pour batter evenly into prepared pans.

3. Bake 30 to 35 minutes or until wooden pick inserted into center comes out clean. Cool 10 minutes; remove from pans to wire racks. Cool completely. Frost with "PERFECTLY CHOCOLATE" CHOCOLATE FROSTING.

One-Pan Cake: Grease and flour 13×9×2-inch baking pan. Heat oven to 350°F. Pour batter into prepared pan. Bake 35 to 40 minutes. Cool completely. Frost.

Three Layer Cake: Grease and flour three 8-inch round baking pans. Heat oven to 350°F. Pour batter into prepared pans. Bake 30 to 35 minutes. Cool 10 minutes; remove from pans to wire racks. Cool completely. Frost.

Bundt Cake: Grease and flour 12-cup fluted tube pan. Heat oven to 350°F. Pour batter into prepared pan. Bake 50 to 55 minutes. Cool 15 minutes; remove from pan to wire rack. Cool completely. Frost.

Cupcakes: Line muffin cups (2½ inches in diameter) with paper bake cups. Heat oven to 350°F. Fill cups ⅔ full with batter. Bake 22 to 25 minutes. Cool completely. Frost. Makes about 30 cupcakes.

"PERFECTLY CHOCOLATE" CHOCOLATE FROSTING

MAKES ABOUT 2 CUPS FROSTING

½ cup (1 stick) butter or margarine

⅔ cup HERSHEY'S Cocoa

3 cups powdered sugar

⅓ cup milk

1 teaspoon vanilla extract

Melt butter. Stir in cocoa. Alternately add powdered sugar and milk, beating to spreading consistency. Add small amount additional milk, if needed. Stir in vanilla. ■

Chocolate Almond Torte

4 eggs, separated

¾ cup sugar, divided

¾ cup ground blanched almonds

⅓ cup all-purpose flour

⅓ cup HERSHEY'S Cocoa

½ teaspoon baking soda

¼ teaspoon salt

¼ cup water

1 teaspoon vanilla extract

¼ teaspoon almond extract

CHERRY FILLING (recipe follows)

CHOCOLATE GLAZE (recipe follows)

Sliced almonds, maraschino cherries or candied cherries, halved

1. Heat oven to 375°F. Grease bottoms of three 8-inch round baking pans. Line bottoms with wax paper; grease paper.

2. Beat egg yolks on medium speed of mixer 3 minutes in medium bowl. Gradually add ½ cup sugar; continue beating 2 minutes. Stir together almonds, flour, cocoa, baking soda and salt; add alternately with water to egg yolk mixture, beating on low speed just until blended. Stir in vanilla and almond extract.

3. Beat egg whites in large bowl until foamy; gradually add remaining ¼ cup sugar, beating until stiff peaks form. Fold small amount beaten egg whites into chocolate mixture; gently fold chocolate mixture into remaining whites just until blended. Spread batter evenly in prepared pans.

4. Bake 16 to 18 minutes or until top springs back when touched lightly in center. Cool 10 minutes; remove from pans to wire racks. Cool completely.

5. Prepare CHERRY FILLING. Place one cake layer on serving plate; spread half of filling over top. Repeat, ending with plain layer on top. Prepare CHOCOLATE GLAZE; spread on top of cake, allowing glaze to run down sides. Garnish with almonds and cherry halves. Refrigerate until glaze is set. Cover; refrigerate leftover torte.

CHERRY FILLING

MAKES ABOUT 2 CUPS FILLING

1 cup (½ pint) cold whipping cream

¼ cup powdered sugar

1½ teaspoons kirsch (cherry brandy) or ¼ teaspoon almond extract

⅓ cup chopped red candied cherries

Beat whipping cream, powdered sugar and brandy until stiff; fold in cherries.

CHOCOLATE GLAZE

MAKES ABOUT ¾ CUP GLAZE

1 tablespoon butter or margarine

2 tablespoons HERSHEY'S Cocoa

2 tablespoons water

1 cup powdered sugar

¼ teaspoon vanilla extract

Melt butter in small saucepan over low heat; add cocoa and water, stirring constantly until slightly thickened. Remove from heat; gradually add powdered sugar and vanilla, beating with whisk until smooth and of spreading consistency. Add additional water, ½ teaspoon at a time, if needed. ■

Chocolate Syrup Swirl Cake

1 cup (2 sticks) butter or margarine, softened

2 cups sugar

2 teaspoons vanilla extract

3 eggs

2¾ cups all-purpose flour

1¼ teaspoons baking soda, divided

½ teaspoon salt

1 cup buttermilk or sour milk*

1 cup HERSHEY'S Syrup

1 cup MOUNDS Sweetened Coconut Flakes (optional)

*To sour milk: Use 1 tablespoon white vinegar plus milk to equal 1 cup.

1. Heat oven to 350°F. Grease and flour 12-cup fluted tube pan or 10-inch tube pan.

2. Beat butter, sugar and vanilla in large bowl until fluffy. Add eggs; beat well. Stir together flour, 1 teaspoon baking soda and salt; add alternately with buttermilk to butter mixture, beating until well blended.

3. Measure 2 cups batter in small bowl; stir in syrup and remaining ¼ teaspoon baking soda. Add coconut, if desired, to remaining vanilla batter; pour into prepared pan. Pour chocolate batter over vanilla batter in pan; do not mix.

4. Bake 60 to 70 minutes or until wooden pick inserted in center comes out clean. Cool 15 minutes; remove from pan to wire rack. Cool completely; glaze or frost as desired. ■

Collector's Cocoa Cake

¾ cup (1½ sticks) butter or margarine, softened

1¾ cups sugar

2 eggs

1 teaspoon vanilla extract

2 cups all-purpose flour

¾ cup HERSHEY'S Cocoa or HERSHEY'S SPECIAL DARK Cocoa

1¼ teaspoons baking soda

½ teaspoon salt

1⅓ cups water

FLUFFY PEANUT BUTTER FROSTING or ONE-BOWL BUTTERCREAM FROSTING (recipes follow)

1. Heat oven to 350°F. Grease and flour two 8- or 9-inch round baking pans.

2. Beat butter and sugar in large bowl until fluffy. Add eggs and vanilla; beat 1 minute on medium speed of mixer. Stir together flour, cocoa, baking soda and salt; add alternately with water to butter mixture, beating until well blended. Pour batter into prepared pans.

3. Bake 35 to 40 minutes for 8-inch layers; 30 to 35 minutes for 9-inch layers or until wooden pick inserted in center comes out clean. Cool 10 minutes; remove from pans to wire racks. Cool completely.

4. Frost with FLUFFY PEANUT BUTTER FROSTING or ONE-BOWL BUTTERCREAM FROSTING.

ONE-BOWL BUTTERCREAM FROSTING

MAKES ABOUT 2 CUPS FROSTING

6 tablespoons butter or margarine, softened

2⅔ cups powdered sugar

½ cup HERSHEY'S Cocoa or HERSHEY'S SPECIAL DARK Cocoa

⅓ cup milk

1 teaspoon vanilla extract

Beat butter in medium bowl. Add powdered sugar and cocoa alternately with milk; beat to spreading consistency (additional milk may be needed). Stir in vanilla.

FLUFFY PEANUT BUTTER FROSTING

MAKES ABOUT 3 CUPS FROSTING

1 cup milk

¼ cup all-purpose flour

1 cup sugar

½ cup REESE'S Creamy Peanut Butter

½ cup shortening

1 teaspoon vanilla extract

Dash salt

1. Gradually stir milk into flour in small saucepan. Cook over low heat, stirring constantly, until very thick. Transfer to medium bowl; press plastic wrap directly on surface. Cool to room temperature, about ½ hour.

2. Add sugar, peanut butter, shortening, vanilla and salt. Beat on high speed of mixer until frosting becomes fluffy and sugar is completely dissolved. ■

Chocolate Cake Fingers

1 cup granulated sugar

1 cup all-purpose flour

⅓ cup HERSHEY'S Cocoa

¾ teaspoon baking powder

¾ teaspoon baking soda

½ cup nonfat milk

¼ cup frozen egg substitute, thawed

¼ cup canola oil or vegetable oil

1 teaspoon vanilla extract

½ cup boiling water

Powdered sugar

1 teaspoon freshly grated orange peel

1½ cups frozen light non-dairy whipped topping, thawed

1. Heat oven to 350°F. Line bottom of 13×9×2-inch baking pan with wax paper.

2. Stir together granulated sugar, flour, cocoa, baking powder and baking soda in large bowl. Add milk, egg substitute, oil and vanilla; beat on medium speed of mixer 2 minutes. Stir in boiling water (batter will be thin). Pour into prepared pan.

3. Bake 16 to 18 minutes or until wooden pick inserted in center comes out clean. With knife or metal spatula, loosen cake from edges of pan. Place clean, lint-free dish towel on wire rack; sprinkle lightly with powdered sugar. Invert cake on towel; peel off wax paper. Cool completely.

4. Invert cake, right side up, on cutting board. Cut cake into small rectangles (about 2×1¼ inches). Stir orange peel into whipped topping; spoon dollop on each piece of cake. Garnish as desired. Store cake, covered, at room temperature. ■

Autumn Peanutty Carrot Cake

3 eggs

¾ cup vegetable oil

1 teaspoon vanilla extract

1½ cups all-purpose flour

¾ cup granulated sugar

½ cup packed light brown sugar

2 teaspoons ground cinnamon

1¼ teaspoons baking soda

2 cups grated carrots

1⅔ cups (10-ounce package) REESE'S Peanut Butter Chips

½ cup chopped walnuts

CREAM CHEESE FROSTING (recipe follows)

1. Heat oven to 350°F. Grease and flour two 8-inch round baking pans.

2. Beat eggs, oil and vanilla in large bowl. Stir together flour, granulated sugar, brown sugar, cinnamon and baking soda; add to egg mixture and blend well. Stir in carrots, peanut butter chips and walnuts; pour into prepared pans.

3. Bake 30 to 35 minutes or until wooden pick inserted in center comes out clean. Cool 10 minutes; remove from pans to wire rack. Cool completely. Frost with CREAM CHEESE FROSTING. Cover; refrigerate leftover cake.

Cream Cheese Frosting: Beat 2 packages (3 ounces each) softened cream cheese and ½ cup (1 stick) softened butter until smooth. Gradually add 4 cups powdered sugar and 2 teaspoons vanilla extract, beating until smooth. ■

Ultra Chocolate Cheesecake

MAKES 12 SERVINGS

MOCHA CRUMB CRUST
(recipe follows)

3 packages (8 ounces each)
cream cheese, softened

1¼ cups sugar

1 container (8 ounces) dairy
sour cream

2 teaspoons vanilla extract

½ cup HERSHEY'S Cocoa

2 tablespoons all-purpose
flour

3 eggs

CHOCOLATE DRIZZLE
(recipe follows)

1. Prepare MOCHA CRUMB CRUST. Heat oven to 350°F.

2. Beat cream cheese and sugar in large bowl until fluffy. Add sour cream and vanilla; beat until blended. Add cocoa and flour; beat until blended. Add eggs; beat well. Pour into crust.

3. Bake 50 to 55 minutes or until set. Remove from oven to wire rack. With knife, loosen cake from side of pan. Cool completely; remove side of pan. Prepare CHOCOLATE DRIZZLE; drizzle over top. Refrigerate 4 to 6 hours. Cover; refrigerate leftover cheesecake.

Chocolate Drizzle:

Place ½ cup HERSHEY'S SPECIAL DARK Chocolate Chips or HERSHEY'S Semi-Sweet Chocolate Chips and 2 teaspoons shortening (do not use butter, margarine, spread or oil) in small microwave-safe bowl. Microwave at MEDIUM (50%) 30 seconds; stir. If necessary, microwave at MEDIUM an additional 10 seconds at a time, stirring after each heating, just until chips are melted and mixture is smooth.

MOCHA CRUMB CRUST

1¼ cups vanilla wafer crumbs (about 40 wafers, crushed)

¼ cup sugar

¼ cup HERSHEY'S Cocoa

1 teaspoon powdered instant espresso or coffee

⅓ cup butter, melted

Heat oven to 350°F. Stir together crumbs, sugar, cocoa and instant espresso in medium bowl. Add butter; stir until well blended. Press mixture firmly onto bottom and 1 inch up side of 9-inch springform pan. Bake 8 minutes; cool slightly. ■

HERSHEY'S® SPECIAL DARK® Chocolate Layered Cheesecake

CHOCOLATE CRUMB CRUST
(recipe follows)

3 packages (8 ounces each)
cream cheese, softened

¾ cup sugar

4 eggs

¼ cup heavy cream

2 teaspoons vanilla extract

¼ teaspoon salt

2 cups (12-ounce package)
HERSHEY'S SPECIAL DARK
Chocolate Chips, divided

½ teaspoon shortening
(do not use butter,
margarine, spread or oil)

1. Prepare CHOCOLATE CRUMB CRUST. Heat oven to 350°F.

2. Beat cream cheese and sugar in large bowl until smooth. Gradually beat in eggs, heavy cream, vanilla and salt, beating until well blended; set aside.

3. Set aside 2 tablespoons chocolate chips. Place remaining chips in large microwave-safe bowl. Microwave at MEDIUM (50%) 1½ minutes; stir. If necessary, microwave at MEDIUM an additional 15 seconds at a time, stirring after each heating, until chocolate is melted when stirred.

4. Gradually blend 1½ cups cheesecake batter into melted chocolate. Spread 2 cups chocolate mixture in prepared crust.

5. Blend another 2 cups plain cheesecake batter into remaining chocolate mixture; spread 2 cups of this mixture over first layer. Stir remaining cheesecake batter into remaining chocolate mixture; spread over second layer.

6. Bake 50 to 55 minutes or until center is almost set. Remove from oven to wire rack. With knife, immediately loosen cake from side of pan. Cool to room temperature.

7. Place reserved chocolate chips and shortening in small microwave-safe bowl. Microwave at MEDIUM 30 seconds; stir. If necessary, microwave at MEDIUM an additional 10 seconds at a time, stirring after each heating, until chocolate is melted and smooth when stirred. Drizzle over top of cheesecake. Cover; refrigerate several hours until cold. Cover and refrigerate leftover cheesecake.

Chocolate Crumb Crust:
Stir together 1½ cups vanilla wafer crumbs (about 45 wafers, crushed), ½ cup powdered sugar and ¼ cup HERSHEY'S Cocoa; stir in ¼ cup (½ stick) melted butter or margarine. Press mixture onto bottom and 1½ inches up sides of 9-inch springform pan. ■

HERSHEY'S® SPECIAL DARK® Truffle Brownie Cheesecake

MAKES 12 SERVINGS

BROWNIE LAYER

6 tablespoons melted butter or margarine

1¼ cups sugar

1 teaspoon vanilla extract

2 eggs

1 cup plus 2 tablespoons all-purpose flour

⅓ cup HERSHEY'S Cocoa

½ teaspoon baking powder

½ teaspoon salt

TRUFFLE CHEESECAKE LAYER

3 packages (8 ounces each) cream cheese, softened

¾ cup sugar

4 eggs

¼ cup heavy cream

2 teaspoons vanilla extract

¼ teaspoon salt

2 cups (12-ounce package) HERSHEY'S SPECIAL DARK Chocolate Chips, divided

½ teaspoon shortening (do not use butter, margarine, spread or oil)

1. Heat oven to 350°F. Grease 9-inch springform pan.

2. For BROWNIE LAYER, stir together melted butter, 1¼ cups sugar and 1 teaspoon vanilla. Add 2 eggs; stir until blended. Stir in flour, cocoa, baking powder and ½ teaspoon salt; blend well. Spread in prepared pan. Bake 25 to 30 minutes or until brownie layer pulls away from sides of pan.

3. Meanwhile for TRUFFLE CHEESECAKE LAYER, beat cream cheese and ¾ cup sugar with mixer on medium speed in large bowl until smooth. Gradually beat in 4 eggs, heavy cream, 2 teaspoons vanilla and ¼ teaspoon salt until well blended.

4. Set aside 2 tablespoons chocolate chips. Place remaining chips in large microwave-safe bowl. Microwave at MEDIUM (50%) 1½ minutes or until chips are melted and smooth when stirred. Gradually blend melted chocolate into cheesecake batter.

5. Remove BROWNIE LAYER from oven and immediately spoon cheesecake mixture over brownie. Return to oven; continue baking 45 to 50 minutes or until center is almost set. Remove from oven to wire rack. With knife, loosen cake from side of pan. Cool to room temperature. Remove side of pan.

6. Place remaining 2 table-spoons chocolate chips and shortening in small microwave-safe bowl. Microwave at MEDIUM 30 seconds or until chips are melted and mixture is smooth when stirred. Drizzle over top of cheesecake. Cover; refrigerate several hours until cold. Garnish as desired. Cover and refrigerate leftover cheesecake. ■

Chilled Raspberry Cheesecake

1½ cups vanilla wafer crumbs (about 45 wafers, crushed)

⅓ cup HERSHEY'S Cocoa

⅓ cup powdered sugar

⅓ cup butter or margarine, melted

1 package (10 ounces) frozen raspberries (about 2½ cups), thawed

1 envelope unflavored gelatin

½ cup cold water

½ cup boiling water

2 packages (8 ounces each) cream cheese, softened

½ cup granulated sugar

1 teaspoon vanilla extract

3 tablespoons seedless red raspberry preserves

CHOCOLATE WHIPPED CREAM (recipe follows)

Fresh raspberries (optional)

Mint leaves (optional)

1. Heat oven to 350°F.

2. Stir together vanilla wafer crumbs, ⅓ cup cocoa and ⅓ cup powdered sugar in medium bowl; stir in melted butter. Press mixture onto bottom and 1½ inches up side of 9-inch springform pan. Bake 10 minutes; cool completely.

3. Purée and strain raspberries; set aside. Sprinkle gelatin over cold water in small bowl; let stand several minutes to soften. Add boiling water; stir until gelatin dissolves completely and mixture is clear. Beat cream cheese, granulated sugar and 1 teaspoon vanilla in large bowl until smooth. Gradually add raspberry purée and gelatin, mixing thoroughly; pour into prepared crust.

4. Refrigerate several hours or overnight. Loosen cake from side of pan with knife; remove side of pan. Stir raspberry preserves to soften; spread over cheesecake top. Garnish with CHOCOLATE WHIPPED CREAM, raspberries and mint, if desired. Cover; refrigerate leftovers.

Chocolate Whipped Cream: Stir together ½ cup powdered sugar and ¼ cup HERSHEY'S Cocoa in medium bowl. Add 1 cup (½ pint) cold whipping cream and 1 teaspoon vanilla extract; beat until stiff. ■

Cappuccino-KISSed Cheesecake

MAKES 12 SERVINGS

1½ cups chocolate cookie crumbs

6 tablespoons butter or margarine, melted

1¼ cups HERSHEY'S MINI KISSES BRAND Milk Chocolates, divided

4 packages (8 ounces each) cream cheese, softened

⅔ cup sugar

3 eggs

⅓ cup milk

1 tablespoon instant espresso powder

¼ teaspoon ground cinnamon

ESPRESSO CREAM (recipe follows)

1. Heat oven to 350°F. Combine cookie crumbs and butter; press onto bottom and 1 inch up side of 9-inch springform pan.

2. Melt 1 cup chocolate pieces in small saucepan over low heat, stirring constantly. Combine cream cheese and sugar in large bowl, beating on medium speed of mixer until well blended. Add eggs, milk, espresso powder and cinnamon; beat on low speed until well blended. Add melted chocolate pieces; beat on medium 2 minutes. Spoon mixture into crust.

3. Bake 55 minutes. Remove from oven to wire rack. Cool 15 minutes; with knife, loosen cake from side of pan. Cool completely; remove side of pan. Cover; refrigerate at least 4 hours before serving.

4. To serve, garnish with ESPRESSO CREAM and remaining ¼ cup chocolates. Cover; refrigerate leftover cheesecake.

Espresso Cream:

Beat ½ cup cold whipping cream, 2 tablespoons powdered sugar and 1 teaspoon instant espresso powder until stiff. ■

Triple Layer Cheesecake

CHOCOLATE CRUMB CRUST
(recipe follows)

3 packages (8 ounces each)
cream cheese, softened

¾ cup sugar

3 eggs

⅓ cup dairy sour cream

3 tablespoons all-purpose
flour

1 teaspoon vanilla extract

¼ teaspoon salt

1 cup HERSHEY'S
Butterscotch Chips, melted*

1 cup HERSHEY'S Premier
White Chips, melted*

1 cup HERSHEY'S SPECIAL
DARK Chocolate Chips or
HERSHEY'S Semi-Sweet
Chocolate Chips, melted*

TRIPLE DRIZZLE (recipe
follows, optional)

*To melt chips: Place chips in
separate medium microwave-safe
bowls. Microwave at MEDIUM
(50%) 1 minute; stir. If necessary,
microwave at MEDIUM an additional
15 seconds at a time, stirring
after each heating, just until
chips are melted when stirred.

1. Heat oven to 350°F. Prepare CHOCOLATE CRUMB CRUST.

2. Beat cream cheese and sugar in large bowl on medium speed of mixer until smooth. Add eggs, sour cream, flour, vanilla and salt; beat until blended. Stir 1⅓ cups batter into melted butterscotch chips until smooth; pour into prepared crust. Stir 1⅓ cups batter into melted white chips until smooth; pour over butterscotch layer. Stir remaining batter into melted chocolate chips until smooth; pour over white layer.

3. Bake 55 to 60 minutes or until almost set in center. Remove from oven to wire rack. With knife, immediately loosen cake from side of pan. Cool completely; remove side of pan. Prepare TRIPLE DRIZZLE, if desired; drizzle, one flavor at a time, over top of cheesecake. Refrigerate about 3 hours. Cover; refrigerate leftover cheesecake.

Chocolate Crumb Crust:
Heat oven to 350°F. Stir together 1½ cups vanilla wafer crumbs (about 45 wafers, crushed), ½ cup powdered sugar and ¼ cup HERSHEY'S Cocoa; stir in ⅓ cup melted butter or margarine. Press mixture onto bottom and 1½ inches up side of 9-inch springform pan. Bake 8 minutes. Cool.

TRIPLE DRIZZLE

1 tablespoon each HERSHEY'S Butterscotch Chips, HERSHEY'S Semi-Sweet Chocolate Chips* and HERSHEY'S Premier White Chips

1½ teaspoons shortening (do not use butter, margarine, spread or oil), divided

*Substitute 1 tablespoon HERSHEY'S SPECIAL DARK Chocolate Chips for HERSHEY'S Semi-Sweet Chocolate Chips, if desired.

Place 1 tablespoon HERSHEY'S Butterscotch Chips and ½ teaspoon shortening in small microwave-safe bowl. Microwave at MEDIUM (50%) 30 to 45 seconds; stir. If necessary, microwave an additional 10 seconds at a time, stirring after each heating, just until chips are melted when stirred. Repeat procedure with 1 tablespoon HERSHEY'S Semi-Sweet Chocolate Chips and HERSHEY'S Premier White Chips. ■

65

Creamy Ambrosia Cheesecake

MAKES 12 SERVINGS

1⅓ cups graham cracker crumbs

½ cup MOUNDS Sweetened Coconut Flakes

¼ cup (½ stick) melted butter or margarine

1¼ cups plus 2 tablespoons sugar, divided

1 can (11 ounces) mandarin orange segments

1 can (8 ounces) crushed pineapple in juice

3 packages (8 ounces each) cream cheese, softened

3 eggs

2 cups (12-ounce package) HERSHEY'S Premier White Chips

TROPICAL FRUIT SAUCE (recipe follows)

Additional MOUNDS Sweetened Coconut Flakes

1. Heat oven to 350°F. Stir graham cracker crumbs, coconut, melted butter and 2 tablespoons sugar in medium bowl. Press mixture firmly onto bottom of 9-inch springform pan. Bake 8 minutes; cool slightly. Drain oranges and pineapple, reserving juices. Chop oranges into small pieces.

2. Beat cream cheese in large bowl until fluffy. Add remaining 1¼ cups sugar; beat well. Add eggs; beat well. Stir in white chips, oranges and pineapple. Pour mixture over crust.

3. Bake 60 to 65 minutes or until center is almost set. Remove from oven to wire rack. With knife, loosen cake from side of pan. Cool completely; remove side of pan. Cover; refrigerate until cold. Garnish with additional coconut, if desired, and serve with TROPICAL FRUIT SAUCE. Cover and refrigerate leftovers.

TROPICAL FRUIT SAUCE

MAKES ABOUT ¾ CUP SAUCE

Juice drained from 1 can (11-ounce-size) mandarin oranges

Juice drained from 1 can (8-ounce-size) crushed pineapple in juice

¼ cup sugar

1 tablespoon cornstarch

¼ teaspoon orange extract or pineapple extract

Combine fruit juices; pour 1 cup combined juice into medium saucepan and discard any remaining juices. Stir in sugar and cornstarch. Cook over medium heat, stirring constantly, until thickened. Remove from heat. Stir in orange extract or pineapple extract. Cool to room temperature before serving. Cover and refrigerate leftover sauce. ■

Classic Chocolate Cream Pie

5 sections (½ ounce each) HERSHEY'S Unsweetened Chocolate Baking Bar, broken into pieces

3 cups milk, divided

1⅓ cups sugar

3 tablespoons all-purpose flour

3 tablespoons cornstarch

½ teaspoon salt

3 egg yolks

2 tablespoons butter or margarine

1½ teaspoons vanilla extract

1 baked (9-inch) pie crust, cooled, or 1 (9-inch) crumb crust

Sweetened whipped cream (optional)

1. Combine chocolate and 2 cups milk in medium saucepan; cook over medium heat, stirring constantly, just until mixture boils. Remove from heat and set aside.

2. Stir together sugar, flour, cornstarch and salt in medium bowl. Whisk remaining 1 cup milk into egg yolks in separate bowl; stir into sugar mixture. Gradually add to chocolate mixture. Cook over medium heat, whisking constantly, until mixture boils; boil and stir 1 minute. Remove from heat; stir in butter and vanilla.

3. Pour into prepared crust; press plastic wrap directly onto surface. Cool; refrigerate until well chilled. Top with whipped cream, if desired. ■

Crispy Chocolate Ice Cream Mud Pie

½ cup HERSHEY'S Syrup

⅓ cup HERSHEY'S SPECIAL DARK Chocolate Chips or HERSHEY'S Semi-Sweet Chocolate Chips

2 cups crisp rice cereal

4 cups (1 quart) vanilla ice cream, divided

4 cups (1 quart) chocolate ice cream, divided

Additional HERSHEY'S Syrup

1. Butter 9-inch pie plate.

2. Place ½ cup chocolate syrup and chocolate chips in medium microwave-safe bowl. Microwave at MEDIUM (50%) 45 seconds or until hot; stir until smooth. Reserve ¼ cup chocolate syrup mixture; set aside. Add cereal to remaining chocolate syrup mixture, stirring until well coated; cool slightly.

3. Press cereal mixture, using back of spoon, evenly on bottom and up side of prepared pie plate to form crust. Place in freezer 15 to 20 minutes or until crust is firm. Spread half of vanilla ice cream into crust; spoon reserved ¼ cup chocolate syrup mixture over layer. Spread half of chocolate ice cream over sauce.

4. Top with alternating scoops of vanilla and chocolate ice cream. Cover; return to freezer until serving time. Drizzle with additional chocolate syrup just before serving. ■

Chocolate Magic Mousse Pie

MAKES 8 SERVINGS

1 envelope unflavored gelatin

2 tablespoons cold water

¼ cup boiling water

1 cup sugar

½ cup HERSHEY'S Cocoa

2 cups (1 pint) cold whipping cream

2 teaspoons vanilla extract

1 packaged (8-inch) graham cracker crumb crust (6 ounces)

Refrigerated light whipped cream in pressurized can or frozen whipped topping, thawed

HERSHEY'S MINI KISSES BRAND Milk Chocolates

1. Sprinkle gelatin over cold water in small bowl; let stand 2 minutes to soften. Add boiling water; stir until gelatin is completely dissolved and mixture is clear. Cool slightly.

2. Mix sugar and cocoa in large bowl; add whipping cream and vanilla. Beat on medium speed, scraping bottom of bowl often, until mixture is stiff. Pour in gelatin mixture; beat until well blended.

3. Spoon into crust. Refrigerate about 3 hours. Garnish with whipped cream and chocolates. Cover; store leftover pie in refrigerator. ■

White Chip Fruit Tart

¾ cup (1½ sticks) butter or margarine, softened

½ cup powdered sugar

1½ cups all-purpose flour

2 cups (12-ounce package) HERSHEY'S Premier White Chips

¼ cup whipping cream

1 package (8 ounces) cream cheese, softened

FRUIT TOPPING (recipe follows)

Assorted fresh fruit, sliced

1. Heat oven to 300°F.

2. Beat butter and powdered sugar in small bowl until smooth; blend in flour. Press mixture onto bottom and up side of 12-inch round pizza pan. Flute edge, if desired.

3. Bake 20 to 25 minutes or until lightly browned; cool completely.

4. Place white chips and whipping cream in medium microwave-safe bowl. Microwave at MEDIUM (50%) 1 to 1½ minutes or until chips are melted and mixture is smooth when stirred. Beat in cream cheese. Spread on cooled crust. Prepare FRUIT TOPPING. Arrange fruit over chip mixture; carefully pour or brush topping over fruit. Cover; refrigerate assembled tart until just before serving.

FRUIT TOPPING

¼ cup sugar

1 tablespoon cornstarch

½ cup pineapple juice

½ teaspoon lemon juice

Stir together sugar and cornstarch in small saucepan; stir in juices. Cook over medium heat, stirring constantly, until thickened; cool. ■

HERSHEY'S® Cocoa Cream Pie

1¼ cups sugar

½ cup HERSHEY'S Cocoa

⅓ cup cornstarch

¼ teaspoon salt

3 cups milk

3 tablespoons butter or margarine

1½ teaspoons vanilla extract

1 baked (9-inch) pie crust, cooled, or 1 (9-inch) graham cracker crumb crust

Sweetened whipped cream

1. Stir together sugar, cocoa, cornstarch and salt in medium saucepan. Gradually add milk, stirring until smooth. Cook over medium heat, stirring constantly, until mixture comes to a boil; boil 1 minute.

2. Remove from heat; stir in butter and vanilla. Pour into prepared crust. Press plastic wrap directly onto surface. Cool to room temperature. Refrigerate 6 to 8 hours. Serve with sweetened whipped cream. Garnish as desired. Cover; refrigerate leftover pie. ∎

REESE'S® Peanut Butter & HERSHEY'S® KISSES® Pie

About 42 HERSHEY'S KISSES BRAND Milk Chocolates, divided

2 tablespoons milk

1 packaged (8-inch) crumb crust (6 ounces)

1 package (8 ounces) cream cheese, softened

¾ cup sugar

1 cup REESE'S Creamy Peanut Butter

1 container (8 ounces) frozen non-dairy whipped topping, thawed and divided

1. Remove wrappers from chocolates. Place 26 chocolates and milk in small microwave-safe bowl. Microwave at MEDIUM (50%) 1 minute or just until melted and smooth when stirred. Spread evenly on bottom of crust. Refrigerate about 30 minutes.

2. Beat cream cheese with mixer on medium speed in medium bowl until smooth; gradually beat in sugar, then peanut butter, beating well after each addition. Reserve ½ cup whipped topping; fold remaining whipped topping into peanut butter mixture. Spoon into crust over chocolate. Cover; refrigerate about 6 hours or until set.

3. Garnish with reserved whipped topping and remaining chocolates. Cover; refrigerate leftover pie. ■

All-Chocolate Boston Cream Pie

1 cup all-purpose flour

1 cup sugar

⅓ cup HERSHEY'S Cocoa

½ teaspoon baking soda

6 tablespoons butter or margarine, softened

1 cup milk

1 egg

1 teaspoon vanilla extract

CHOCOLATE FILLING (recipe follows)

SATINY CHOCOLATE GLAZE (recipe follows)

1. Heat oven to 350°F. Grease and flour one 9-inch round baking pan.

2. Stir together flour, sugar, cocoa and baking soda in large bowl. Add butter, milk, egg and vanilla. Beat on low speed of mixer until all ingredients are moistened. Beat on medium speed 2 minutes. Pour batter into prepared pan.

3. Bake 30 to 35 minutes or until wooden pick inserted in center comes out clean. Cool 10 minutes; remove from pan to wire rack. Cool completely. Prepare CHOCOLATE FILLING. Cut cake into two thin layers. Place one layer on serving plate; spread filling over layer. Top with remaining layer.

4. Prepare SATINY CHOCOLATE GLAZE. Pour onto top of cake, allowing some to drizzle down sides. Refrigerate until serving time. Cover; refrigerate leftover cake.

CHOCOLATE FILLING

½ cup sugar

¼ cup HERSHEY'S Cocoa

2 tablespoons cornstarch

1½ cups light cream

1 tablespoon butter or margarine

1 teaspoon vanilla extract

Stir together sugar, cocoa and cornstarch in medium saucepan; gradually stir in light cream. Cook over medium heat, stirring constantly, until mixture thickens and begins to boil. Boil 1 minute, stirring constantly; remove from heat. Stir in butter and vanilla. Press plastic wrap directly onto surface. Cool completely.

SATINY CHOCOLATE GLAZE

2 tablespoons water

1 tablespoon butter or margarine

1 tablespoon corn syrup

2 tablespoons HERSHEY'S Cocoa

¾ cup powdered sugar

½ teaspoon vanilla extract

Heat water, butter and corn syrup in small saucepan to boiling. Remove from heat; immediately stir in cocoa. With whisk, gradually beat in powdered sugar and vanilla until smooth; cool slightly. ∎

Chocolate Marbled Peanut Butter Pie

½ cup REESE'S Creamy Peanut Butter

1 package (3 ounces) cream cheese, softened

½ teaspoon vanilla extract

1 cup powdered sugar

½ cup milk

1 container (8 ounces) frozen non-dairy whipped topping, thawed

1 extra serving-size packaged graham crumb crust (9 ounces)

½ cup HERSHEY'S SPECIAL DARK Chocolate Chips or HERSHEY'S Semi-Sweet Chocolate Chips

1. Beat peanut butter, cream cheese and vanilla in medium bowl on medium speed of mixer until smooth. Gradually add powdered sugar and milk, beating until smooth. Fold in whipped topping. Place 1 cup peanut butter mixture in separate bowl. Spread remaining mixture in crust.

2. Place chocolate chips in small microwave-safe bowl. Microwave at MEDIUM (50%) 30 seconds or until chocolate is melted and smooth when stirred. Stir chocolate into reserved peanut butter mixture, blending thoroughly; drop by tablespoons onto top of pie. Using knife or spatula, gently swirl for marbled effect.

3. Cover; freeze 4 to 5 hours or until firm. Garnish as desired. ■

Deep Dark Mousse

¼ cup sugar

1 teaspoon unflavored gelatin

½ cup milk

1 cup HERSHEY'S SPECIAL DARK Chocolate Chips

2 teaspoons vanilla extract

1 cup (½ pint) cold whipping cream

Sweetened whipped cream (optional)

1. Stir together sugar and gelatin in small saucepan; stir in milk. Let stand 2 minutes to soften gelatin. Cook over medium heat, stirring constantly, until mixture just begins to boil.

2. Remove from heat. Immediately add chocolate chips; stir until melted. Stir in vanilla; cool to room temperature.

3. Beat whipping cream with mixer on high speed in medium bowl until stiff peaks form. Add half of chocolate mixture and gently fold until nearly combined; add remaining chocolate mixture and fold just until blended. Spoon into serving dish or individual dishes. Refrigerate. Garnish with sweetened whipped cream, if desired, just before serving. ■

Pears with Chocolate-Orange Sauce

6 fresh pears

1½ cups apple juice

1 teaspoon vanilla extract

CHOCOLATE-ORANGE SAUCE (recipe follows)

1. Slice piece off bottom of pears to make a flat base. Peel pears and core from bottom but leave stems intact.

2. Combine juice with vanilla in large saucepan; add pears, base side down. Heat to boiling; reduce heat. Cover; simmer, spooning juice over pears occasionally, 20 to 25 minutes or until pears are tender.

3. Meanwhile, prepare CHOCOLATE-ORANGE SAUCE. To serve, place pear, base side down, in serving dish; spoon about 1 tablespoon warm sauce over top.

CHOCOLATE-ORANGE SAUCE

MAKES ½ CUP SAUCE

¾ cup HERSHEY'S SPECIAL DARK Chocolate Chips or HERSHEY'S Semi-Sweet Chocolate Chips

1 tablespoon shortening (do not use butter, margarine, spread or oil)

¼ teaspoon orange extract

Place all ingredients in medium microwave-safe bowl. Microwave at MEDIUM (50%) 30 seconds; stir. If necessary, microwave at MEDIUM an additional 10 seconds at a time, stirring after each heating, until chocolate is melted and mixture is smooth when stirred. Serve warm sauce over hot poached pears. ■

Cherry Glazed Chocolate Torte

½ cup (1 stick) butter or margarine, melted

1 cup granulated sugar

1 teaspoon vanilla extract

2 eggs

½ cup all-purpose flour

⅓ cup HERSHEY'S Cocoa

¼ teaspoon baking powder

¼ teaspoon salt

1 package (8 ounces) cream cheese, softened

1 cup powdered sugar

1 cup frozen non-dairy whipped topping, thawed

1 can (21 ounces) cherry pie filling, divided

1. Heat oven to 350°F. Grease bottom of 9-inch springform pan.

2. Stir together butter, granulated sugar and vanilla in large bowl. Add eggs; using spoon, beat well. Stir together flour, cocoa, baking powder and salt; gradually add to egg mixture, beating until well blended. Spread batter in prepared pan.

3. Bake 25 to 30 minutes or until cake is set. (Cake will be fudgey and will not test done.) Remove from oven; cool completely in pan on wire rack.

4. Beat cream cheese and powdered sugar in medium bowl until well blended; gradually fold in whipped topping, blending well. Spread over top of cake. Spread 1 cup cherry pie filling over cream layer; refrigerate several hours. With knife, loosen cake from side of pan; remove side of pan. Cut into wedges; garnish with remaining pie filling. Cover; refrigerate leftover dessert. ■

Easy Chocoberry Cream Dessert

MAKES 12 SERVINGS

2 packages (3 ounces each) ladyfingers, split

1 package (10 ounces) frozen strawberries in syrup, thawed and drained

2 envelopes unflavored gelatin

2 cups milk, divided

1 cup sugar

⅓ cup HERSHEY'S Cocoa or HERSHEY'S SPECIAL DARK Cocoa

¼ cup (½ stick) butter or margarine

1 teaspoon vanilla extract

2 cups frozen non-dairy whipped topping, thawed

Additional whipped topping (optional)

Fresh strawberries (optional)

Mint leaves (optional)

1. Place ladyfingers, cut side in, on bottom and around sides of 9-inch springform pan.

2. Purée strawberries in food processor. Sprinkle gelatin over 1 cup milk in medium saucepan; let stand 2 minutes to soften. Add sugar, cocoa and butter. Cook over medium heat, stirring constantly, until mixture is hot and gelatin is completely dissolved. Remove from heat; stir in remaining 1 cup milk, vanilla and puréed strawberries. Refrigerate until mixture begins to thicken.

3. Fold 2 cups whipped topping into gelatin mixture. Pour mixture into prepared pan. Cover; refrigerate until mixture is firm. Just before serving, remove side of pan. Garnish with additional whipped topping, fresh strawberries and mint, if desired. Cover; refrigerate leftover dessert. ■

Milk Chocolate Pots de Crème

2 cups (11.5-ounce package) HERSHEY'S Milk Chocolate Chips

½ cup light cream

½ teaspoon vanilla extract

Sweetened whipped cream (optional)

1. Place milk chocolate chips and light cream in medium microwave-safe bowl. Microwave at MEDIUM (50%) 1 minute; stir. If necessary, microwave at MEDIUM an additional 15 seconds at a time, stirring after each heating, just until chocolate is melted and smooth when stirred. Stir in vanilla.

2. Pour into demitasse cups or very small dessert dishes. Cover; refrigerate until firm. Serve cold with sweetened whipped cream, if desired. ■

Peanut Butter Fondue

Selection of fruits and other fondue dippers

3⅓ cups (two 10-ounce packages) REESE'S Peanut Butter Chips

1½ cups light cream

1. Prepare ahead of time a selection of fresh fruit chunks for dipping: apples, bananas, pears, peaches, cherries, pineapple, oranges (brush fresh fruit with lemon juice to prevent browning). Cover; refrigerate until ready to serve. (Dried apples and apricots, marshmallows and bite-size pieces of pound cake can also be used for dipping.)

2. Place peanut butter chips and light cream in medium microwave-safe bowl. Microwave at MEDIUM (50%) 11⁄2 minutes; stir. If necessary, microwave at MEDIUM an additional 30 seconds at a time, stirring after each heating, until chips are melted and mixture is smooth when stirred.

3. Pour into fondue pot; keep warm over low heat. Dip chunks of fruit into warm sauce with forks. Keep leftover sauce covered and refrigerated.

Note: Recipe may be halved using 1 package (10 ounces) REESE'S Peanut Butter Chips and ¾ cup light cream.■

Chocolate Syrup Swirl Dessert

CRUMB CRUST
(recipe follows)

1 envelope unflavored
gelatin

¼ cup cold water

1 package (8 ounces)
cream cheese, softened

¼ cup sugar

1 teaspoon vanilla extract

¾ cup HERSHEY'S
Syrup, chilled

¾ cup milk

VANILLA FILLING
(recipe follows)

Additional HERSHEY'S
Syrup (optional)

1. Prepare CRUMB CRUST.

2. Sprinkle gelatin over water in small saucepan; let stand 2 minutes. Cook over low heat, stirring constantly, until gelatin is dissolved.

3. Beat cream cheese, sugar and vanilla in large bowl until creamy. Add syrup, gelatin mixture and milk; blend well. Refrigerate, stirring occasionally, until mixture mounds from spoon, about 20 minutes.

4. Spoon one-half chocolate mixture into prepared crust; top with one-half VANILLA FILLING. Repeat procedure, ending with spoonfuls of VANILLA FILLING on top. Using knife or metal spatula, gently swirl through dessert. Cover; refrigerate several hours until set. Serve with additional syrup, if desired.

Crumb Crust: Stir together 2 cups vanilla wafer crumbs (about 60 wafers, crushed) and ⅓ cup melted butter or margarine in medium bowl. Press mixture onto bottom and 1½ inches up side of 9-inch springform pan or 10-inch pie plate. Refrigerate about 30 minutes or until firm.

VANILLA FILLING

1 teaspoon unflavored gelatin

1 tablespoon cold water

2 tablespoons boiling water

1 cup (½ pint) cold whipping cream

2 tablespoons sugar

½ teaspoon vanilla extract

Sprinkle gelatin over cold water in small cup; let stand 1 minute. Add boiling water; stir until gelatin is completely dissolved; cool slightly. Combine whipping cream, sugar and vanilla in medium bowl; beat until slightly thickened. Gradually add gelatin mixture; beat until stiff. ■

White & Chocolate Covered Strawberries

MAKES ABOUT 3 DOZEN BERRIES

2 cups (12-ounce package) HERSHEY'S Premier White Chips

2 tablespoons shortening (do not use butter, margarine, spread or oil), divided

4 cups (2 pints) fresh strawberries, rinsed, patted dry and chilled

1 cup HERSHEY'S SPECIAL DARK Chocolate Chips or HERSHEY'S Semi-Sweet Chocolate Chips

1. Cover tray with wax paper.

2. Place white chips and 1 tablespoon shortening in medium microwave-safe bowl. Microwave at MEDIUM (50%) 1 minute; stir until chips are melted and mixture is smooth. If necessary, microwave at MEDIUM an additional 15 seconds at a time, just until smooth when stirred.

3. Holding by top, dip one third of each strawberry into white chip mixture; shake gently to remove excess. Place on prepared tray; refrigerate until coating is firm, at least 30 minutes.

4. Repeat microwave procedure with chocolate chips and remaining shortening in clean microwave-safe bowl. Dip lower one third of each berry into chocolate mixture. Refrigerate until firm. Cover; refrigerate leftover strawberries. ■

REESE'S® Peanut Butter Bark

2 packages (4 ounces each) HERSHEY'S Semi-Sweet Chocolate Baking Bars, broken into pieces

1⅔ cups (10-ounce package) REESE'S Peanut Butter Chips

1 tablespoon shortening (do not use butter, margarine, spread or oil)

½ cup roasted peanuts or toasted almonds,* coarsely chopped

*To toast almonds: Heat oven to 350°F. Spread almonds in thin layer in shallow baking pan. Bake 8 to 10 minutes, stirring occasionally, until light golden brown; cool.

1. Cover tray with wax paper.

2. Place chocolate in medium microwave-safe bowl. Microwave at MEDIUM (50%) 1 minute; stir. If necessary, microwave at MEDIUM an additional 15 seconds at a time, stirring after each heating, until chocolate is melted and smooth when stirred.

3. Immediately place peanut butter chips and shortening in second microwave-safe bowl. Microwave at MEDIUM 1 minute; stir. If necessary, microwave at MEDIUM an additional 15 seconds at a time, stirring after each heating, until chips are melted and mixture is smooth when stirred; stir in peanuts.

4. Alternately spoon above mixtures onto prepared tray; swirl with knife for marbled effect. Gently tap tray on countertop to even thickness of mixture. Cover; refrigerate until firm. Break into pieces. Store in cool, dry place. ■

Chocolate and Orange Meltaways

2 cups (12-ounce package) HERSHEY'S Premier White Chips, divided

½ cup (1 stick) unsalted butter (do not substitute margarine)

⅓ cup whipping cream

1½ teaspoons orange extract

CHOCOLATE COATING (recipe follows)

½ teaspoon shortening (do not use butter, margarine, spread or oil)

1. Line tray with wax paper. Reserve 2 tablespoons white chips.

2. Combine butter and whipping cream in medium saucepan; cook over low heat, stirring constantly until mixture comes to a full rolling boil. Remove from heat; immediately add remaining white chips. Stir with whisk until smooth. Add orange extract; blend well.

3. Refrigerate until firm enough to handle, about 2 hours. Taking small amount of mixture at a time, shape into 1-inch balls. Place on prepared tray; refrigerate until firm, about 1½ hours. Prepare CHOCOLATE COATING. Place one candy onto fork; dip into coating, covering completely and allowing excess to drip off. Place candies onto prepared tray. Repeat with remaining candies. Refrigerate until coating is set, about 1 hour.

4. Place reserved 2 tablespoons white chips and shortening in small microwave-safe bowl. Microwave at MEDIUM (50%) 30 seconds; stir. If necessary, microwave at MEDIUM an additional 10 seconds or until mixture is smooth when stirred. With fork, lightly drizzle over coated candies; refrigerate until set, about 20 minutes. Cover; store in refrigerator.

Chocolate Coating:

Place 2 packages (4 ounces each) HERSHEY'S Semi-Sweet Chocolate Baking Bars, broken into pieces, and 1 teaspoon shortening (do not use butter, margarine, spread or oil) in medium microwave-safe bowl. Microwave at MEDIUM (50%) 2 minutes; stir. If necessary, microwave at MEDIUM an additional 15 seconds at a time, stirring after each heating, until chocolate is melted and mixture is smooth when stirred. Cool slightly. (If chocolate is too hot, it will not coat candy.) ■

KISSES® Fluted Cups with Peanut Butter Filling

MAKES ABOUT 2 DOZEN PIECES

72 HERSHEY'S KISSESBRAND Milk Chocolates, divided

1 cup REESE'S Creamy Peanut Butter

1 cup powdered sugar

1 tablespoon butter or margarine, softened

1. Line 24 small muffin cups (1¾ inches in diameter) with small paper bake cups. Remove wrappers from chocolates.

2. Place 48 chocolates in small microwave-safe bowl. Microwave at MEDIUM (50%) 1 minute; stir. Microwave at MEDIUM an additional 10 seconds at a time, stirring after each heating, just until chocolate is melted when stirred. Using small brush, coat inside of paper cups with melted chocolate.

3. Refrigerate 20 minutes; reapply melted chocolate to any thin spots. Refrigerate until firm, preferably overnight. Gently peel paper from chocolate cups.

4. Beat peanut butter, powdered sugar and butter with electric mixer on medium speed in small bowl until smooth. Spoon into chocolate cups. Before serving, top each cup with a chocolate piece. Cover; store cups in refrigerator. ◼

Chocolate-Covered Banana Pops

MAKES 9 POPS

3 ripe large bananas

9 wooden ice cream sticks

2 cups (12-ounce package) HERSHEY'S SPECIAL DARK Chocolate Chips or HERSHEY'S Semi-Sweet Chocolate Chips

2 tablespoons shortening (do not use butter, margarine, spread or oil)

1½ cups coarsely chopped unsalted, roasted peanuts

1. Peel bananas; cut each into thirds. Insert a wooden stick into each banana piece; place on wax paper-covered tray. Cover; freeze until firm.

2. Place chocolate chips and shortening in medium microwave-safe bowl. Microwave at MEDIUM (50%) 1½ to 2 minutes or until chocolate is melted and mixture is smooth when stirred.

3. Remove bananas from freezer just before dipping. Dip each piece into warm chocolate, covering completely; allow excess to drip off. Immediately roll in peanuts. Cover; return to freezer. Serve frozen.

Variation: HERSHEY'S Milk Chocolate Chips or HERSHEY'S Mini Chips Semi-Sweet Chocolate may be substituted for HERSHEY'S SPECIAL DARK Chocolate Chips or HERSHEY'S Semi-Sweet Chocolate Chips. ■

Filled Chocolate Meringues

2 egg whites, at room temperature

¼ teaspoon cream of tartar

Dash salt

½ cup sugar

½ teaspoon vanilla extract

2 tablespoons HERSHEY'S Cocoa

CHOCOLATE-CHEESE FILLING (recipe follows)

Raspberries and mint leaves for garnish

1. Heat oven to 275°F. Place parchment paper on cookie sheets.

2. Beat egg whites with cream of tartar and salt in medium bowl until soft peaks form. Beat in sugar, 1 tablespoon at a time, until stiff, glossy peaks form. Fold in vanilla. Sift cocoa over top of egg white mixture; gently fold in cocoa until combined. Drop by tablespoonfuls onto parchment paper. With back of small spoon, make indentation in center of each mound.

3. Bake 45 minutes or until meringue turns a light cream color and feels dry to the touch. Cool slightly; carefully peel meringues off parchment paper; cool completely on wire racks. To serve, spoon or pipe about 2 teaspoons CHOCOLATE-CHEESE FILLING into center of each meringue. Garnish each with a raspberry and a mint leaf.

Chocolate-Cheese Filling: Combine 1 cup part-skim ricotta cheese, 2 tablespoons HERSHEY'S Cocoa, 1 tablespoon sugar and ½ teaspoon vanilla extract in food processor; blend until smooth. Cover; refrigerate. Makes 1 cup filling. ■

HERSHEY'S® KISSES® Birthday Cake

2 cups sugar

1¾ cups all-purpose flour

¾ cup HERSHEY'S Cocoa or HERSHEY'S SPECIAL DARK Cocoa

1½ teaspoons baking powder

1½ teaspoons baking soda

1 teaspoon salt

2 eggs

1 cup milk

½ cup vegetable oil

2 teaspoons vanilla extract

1 cup boiling water

VANILLA BUTTERCREAM FROSTING (recipe follows)

HERSHEY'S KISSESBRAND Milk Chocolates

1. Heat oven to 350°F. Grease and flour two (9-inch) round baking pans or one (13×9×2-inch) baking pan.

2. Stir together sugar, flour, cocoa, baking powder, baking soda and salt in large bowl. Add eggs, milk, oil and vanilla; beat with mixer on medium speed for 2 minutes. Stir in boiling water (batter will be thin). Pour batter into prepared pans.

3. Bake 30 to 35 minutes for round pans, 35 to 40 minutes for rectangular pan or until wooden pick inserted in center comes out clean. Cool 10 minutes; turn out onto wire racks. Cool completely.

4. Frost with VANILLA BUTTERCREAM FROSTING. Remove wrappers from chocolates. Garnish top and sides of cake with chocolates.

VANILLA BUTTERCREAM FROSTING

MAKES ABOUT
2⅓ CUPS FROSTING

⅓ cup butter or margarine, softened

4 cups powdered sugar, divided

3 to 4 tablespoons milk

1½ teaspoons vanilla extract

Beat butter with electric mixer on medium speed in large bowl until creamy. With mixer running, gradually add about 2 cups powdered sugar, beating until well blended. Slowly beat in milk and vanilla. Gradually add remaining powdered sugar, beating until smooth. Add additional milk, if necessary, until frosting is desired consistency. ■

HERSHEY'S® White and Dark Chocolate Fudge Torte

MAKES 12 SERVINGS

1 cup (2 sticks) butter or margarine, melted

1½ cups sugar

1 teaspoon vanilla extract

3 eggs, separated

⅔ cup HERSHEY'S Cocoa

½ cup all-purpose flour

3 tablespoons water

2 cups (12-ounce package) HERSHEY'S Premier White Chips, divided

⅛ teaspoon cream of tartar

SATINY GLAZE (recipe follows)

WHITE DECORATOR DRIZZLE (recipe follows)

1. Heat oven to 350°F. Line bottom of 9-inch springform pan with foil; grease foil and side of pan.

2. Combine butter, sugar and vanilla in large bowl; beat well. Add egg yolks, one at a time, beating well after each addition. Blend in cocoa, flour and water. Stir in 1⅔ cups white chips. Reserve remaining chips for drizzle. Beat egg whites with cream of tartar in small bowl until stiff peaks form; fold into chocolate mixture. Pour batter into prepared pan.

3. Bake 45 minutes or until top begins to crack slightly. (Cake will not test done in center.) Cool 1 hour. Cover; refrigerate until firm. Remove side of pan. Prepare SATINY GLAZE and WHITE DECORATOR DRIZZLE. Pour prepared glaze over torte; spread evenly over top and sides. Decorate top of torte with prepared drizzle* or wait to prepare drizzle and decorate individual slices before serving. Cover; refrigerate until serving time. Refrigerate leftover torte.

*To decorate, drizzle with spoon or place in pastry bag with writing tip.

SATINY GLAZE
MAKES ABOUT ¾ CUP GLAZE

1 cup HERSHEY'S SPECIAL DARK Chocolate Chips or HERSHEY'S Semi-Sweet Chocolate Chips

¼ cup whipping cream

Place chocolate chips and whipping cream in small microwave-safe bowl. Microwave at MEDIUM (50%) 1 minute; stir. If necessary, microwave at MEDIUM an additional 15 seconds at a time, stirring after each heating, just until chips are melted when stirred. Cool until lukewarm and slightly thickened.

WHITE DECORATOR DRIZZLE

⅓ cup HERSHEY'S Premier White Chips (reserved from torte)

2 teaspoons shortening (do not use butter, margarine, spread or oil)

Place white chips and shortening in small microwave-safe bowl. Microwave at MEDIUM (50%) 20 to 30 seconds; stir. If necessary, microwave at MEDIUM an additional 10 seconds at a time, stirring after each heating, just until chips are melted when stirred. ■

Holiday Coconut Cake

½ cup (1 stick) butter or margarine, softened

½ cup shortening

2 cups sugar

5 eggs, separated

1 teaspoon vanilla extract

2 cups all-purpose flour

1 teaspoon baking soda

¼ teaspoon salt

1 cup buttermilk

2 cups MOUNDS Sweetened Coconut Flakes

½ cup chopped pecans

TOFFEE CREAM (recipe follows)

Additional HEATH BITS 'O BRICKLE Toffee Bits (optional)

1. Heat oven to 350°F. Grease and flour 12-cup fluted tube pan.

2. Beat butter, shortening, sugar, egg yolks and vanilla with mixer on medium speed in large bowl until creamy. Stir together flour, baking soda and salt; add alternately with buttermilk, beating until well blended. Stir in coconut and pecans.

3. Beat egg whites with electric mixer on high speed in large bowl until stiff peaks form; fold into batter. Pour batter into prepared pan.

4. Bake 45 to 55 minutes or until wooden pick inserted in center comes out clean. Cool 10 minutes; remove from pan to wire rack. Cool completely. Frost cake with TOFFEE CREAM. Garnish with additional toffee bits, if desired. Cover; store leftover cake in refrigerator.

Toffee Cream: Beat 2 cups (1 pint) whipping cream with ¼ cup powdered sugar and 1 teaspoon vanilla extract in large bowl until stiff peaks form. Fold in ½ cup HEATH BITS 'O BRICKLE Toffee Bits. Makes about 4 cups. ■

KISSES® & Peanut Butter Cup Easter Pie

MAKES 8 SERVINGS

16 REESE'S Peanut Butter Cups Miniatures, unwrapped and chopped

5¼ cups (12 ounces) frozen non-dairy whipped topping, thawed and divided

2 tablespoons REESE'S Creamy Peanut Butter

1 prepared (6-ounce) graham cracker crumb crust

27 HERSHEY'S KISSESBRAND Milk Chocolates, unwrapped

24 REESE'S Peanut Butter Cups Miniatures or HERSHEY'S KISSESBRAND Milk Chocolates, unwrapped

24 HERSHEY'S Candy-Coated Milk Chocolate Eggs

1. Combine chopped peanut butter cups, 2 cups whipped topping and peanut butter in large bowl. Spread onto bottom of crumb crust.

2. Place 27 milk chocolate pieces in small microwave-safe bowl. Microwave at MEDIUM (50%) 1 minute; stir. If necessary, microwave at MEDIUM an additional 15 seconds at a time, stirring after each heating, until chocolate is melted and smooth when stirred. Stir in 2 cups whipped topping; spread on top of peanut butter layer. Cover; refrigerate until firm.

3. Spread remaining 1¼ cups whipped topping on top of pie. Cut into slices and decorate each slice with 3 candies and 3 candy eggs. Serve immediately; refrigerate leftovers. ■

MINI KISSES® Pumpkin Mousse Cups

MAKES 10 SERVINGS

1¾ cups
(10-ounce package)
HERSHEY'S MINI
KISSESBRAND Milk
Chocolates, divided

24 large marshmallows

½ cup milk

½ cup canned pumpkin

1 teaspoon vanilla extract

1 teaspoon pumpkin
pie spice

⅓ cup powdered sugar

1 cup (½ pint) cold
whipping cream

Additional sweetened
whipped cream (optional)

1. Line 10 muffin cups (2½ inches in diameter) with paper bake cups. Reserve ½ cup chocolate pieces. Place remaining 1¼ cups chocolates in small microwave-safe bowl; microwave at MEDIUM (50%) 1 minute or until melted when stirred. Mixture should be thick.

2. Very thickly coat inside pleated surfaces and bottoms of bake cups with melted chocolate using soft pastry brush. Refrigerate 10 minutes; recoat any thin spots with melted chocolate.* Refrigerate until firm, about 2 hours. Gently peel off paper; refrigerate until ready to fill.

3. Place marshmallows, milk and pumpkin in medium microwave-safe bowl. Microwave at MEDIUM 1 minute; stir. Microwave additional 30 seconds at a time, stirring after each heating, until mixture is melted and smooth. Stir in vanilla and pumpkin pie spice. Cool completely.

4. Beat powdered sugar and whipping cream until stiff; fold into pumpkin mixture. Fill cups with pumpkin mousse; garnish with reserved chocolate pieces and sweetened whipped cream, if desired. Cover; refrigerate 2 hours or until firm. ■

*If reheating is needed, microwave chocolate at MEDIUM 15 seconds; stir.

SPECIAL DARK® Chocolate Chip Scones

MAKES 24 SCONES

3¼ cups all-purpose flour

½ cup granulated sugar

1 tablespoon plus
1 teaspoon baking powder

¼ teaspoon salt

2 cups (12-ounce package)
HERSHEY'S SPECIAL DARK
Chocolate Chips

½ cup chopped nuts
(optional)

2 cups whipping cream,
chilled

2 tablespoons butter,
melted

Additional granulated sugar

Powdered sugar (optional)

1. Heat oven to 375°F. Lightly grease 2 baking sheets.

2. Stir together flour, ½ cup granulated sugar, baking powder and salt in large bowl. Stir in chocolate chips and nuts, if desired.

3. Stir whipping cream into flour mixture just until ingredients are moistened.

4. Turn mixture out onto lightly floured surface. Knead gently until soft dough forms, about 2 minutes. Divide dough into three equal balls. One ball at a time, flatten into 7-inch circle; cut into 8 triangles. Transfer triangles to prepared baking sheets, spacing 2 inches apart. Brush with melted butter and sprinkle with additional granulated sugar.

5. Bake 15 to 20 minutes or until lightly browned. Serve warm, sprinkled with powdered sugar, if desired. ■

Holiday Chocolate Cake

MAKES 12 SERVINGS

2 cups sugar

1¾ cups all-purpose flour

¾ cup HERSHEY'S Cocoa

2 teaspoons baking soda

1 teaspoon baking powder

1 teaspoon salt

1 cup buttermilk or sour milk*

1 cup strong black coffee or 2 teaspoons powdered instant coffee dissolved in 1 cup hot water

½ cup vegetable oil

2 eggs

2 teaspoons vanilla extract

RICOTTA CHEESE FILLING (recipe follows)

CHOCOLATE WHIPPED CREAM (recipe follows)

VANILLA WHIPPED CREAM (recipe follows)

Candied red or green cherries (optional)

*To sour milk: Use 1 tablespoon white vinegar plus milk to equal 1 cup.

1. Heat oven to 350°F. Grease and flour two 9-inch round baking pans.

2. Stir together sugar, flour, cocoa, baking soda, baking powder and salt in large bowl. Add buttermilk, coffee, oil, eggs and vanilla; beat at medium speed of mixer 2 minutes (batter will be thin). Pour batter into prepared pans.

3. Bake 30 to 35 minutes or until wooden pick inserted into center of cakes come out clean. Cool 10 minutes; remove from pans to wire racks. Cool completely.

4. Slice cake layers in half horizontally. Place bottom slice on serving plate; top with ⅓ RICOTTA CHEESE FILLING. Alternate cake layers and filling, ending with cake on top. Frost cake with CHOCOLATE WHIPPED CREAM. Decorate with VANILLA WHIPPED CREAM and cherries, if desired. Cover; refrigerate leftover cake.

Chocolate Whipped Cream: Stir together ⅓ cup powdered sugar and 2 tablespoons HERSHEY'S Cocoa in small bowl. Add 1 cup (½ pint) cold whipping cream and 1 teaspoon vanilla extract; beat until stiff.

Vanilla Whipped Cream: Beat ½ cup cold whipping cream, 2 tablespoons powdered sugar and ½ teaspoon vanilla extract in small bowl until stiff.

RICOTTA CHEESE FILLING

1¾ cups (15 ounces) ricotta cheese*

¼ cup sugar

3 tablespoons Grand Marnier (orange-flavored liqueur) or orange juice concentrate, undiluted

¼ cup candied red or green cherries, coarsely chopped

⅓ cup HERSHEY'S Mini Chips Semi-Sweet Chocolate

*1 cup (½ pint) whipping cream can be substituted for ricotta cheese. Beat with sugar and liqueur until stiff.

Beat ricotta cheese, sugar and liqueur in large bowl until smooth. Fold in candied cherries and small chocolate chips. ∎

Holiday Red Raspberry Chocolate Bars

MAKES 24 BARS

2½ cups all-purpose flour

1 cup sugar

¾ cup finely chopped pecans

1 egg, beaten

1 cup (2 sticks) cold butter or margarine

1 jar (12 ounces) seedless red raspberry jam

1⅔ cups HERSHEY'S Milk Chocolate Chips, HERSHEY'S SPECIAL DARK Chocolate Chips, HERSHEY'S Semi-Sweet Chocolate Chips or HERSHEY'S MINI KISSES BRAND Milk Chocolates

1. Heat oven to 350°F. Grease 13×9×2-inch baking pan.

2. Stir together flour, sugar, pecans and egg in large bowl. Cut in butter with pastry blender or fork until mixture resembles coarse crumbs; set aside 1½ cups crumb mixture. Press remaining crumb mixture on bottom of prepared pan. Stir jam to soften; carefully spread over crumb mixture in pan. Sprinkle with chocolate chips. Crumble reserved crumb mixture evenly over top.

3. Bake 40 to 45 minutes or until lightly browned. Cool completely in pan on wire rack; cut into bars. ■

INDEX

INDEX

INDEX

METRIC CONVERSION CHART

VOLUME MEASUREMENTS (dry)

$^1/_8$ teaspoon = 0.5 mL
$^1/_4$ teaspoon = 1 mL
$^1/_2$ teaspoon = 2 mL
$^3/_4$ teaspoon = 4 mL
1 teaspoon = 5 mL
1 tablespoon = 15 mL
2 tablespoons = 30 mL
$^1/_4$ cup = 60 mL
$^1/_3$ cup = 75 mL
$^1/_2$ cup = 125 mL
$^2/_3$ cup = 150 mL
$^3/_4$ cup = 175 mL
1 cup = 250 mL
2 cups = 1 pint = 500 mL
3 cups = 750 mL
4 cups = 1 quart = 1 L

VOLUME MEASUREMENTS (fluid)

1 fluid ounce (2 tablespoons) = 30 mL
4 fluid ounces ($^1/_2$ cup) = 125 mL
8 fluid ounces (1 cup) = 250 mL
12 fluid ounces (1$^1/_2$ cups) = 375 mL
16 fluid ounces (2 cups) = 500 mL

WEIGHTS (mass)

$^1/_2$ ounce = 15 g
1 ounce = 30 g
3 ounces = 90 g
4 ounces = 120 g
8 ounces = 225 g
10 ounces = 285 g
12 ounces = 360 g
16 ounces = 1 pound = 450 g

DIMENSIONS

$^1/_{16}$ inch = 2 mm
$^1/_8$ inch = 3 mm
$^1/_4$ inch = 6 mm
$^1/_2$ inch = 1.5 cm
$^3/_4$ inch = 2 cm
1 inch = 2.5 cm

OVEN TEMPERATURES

250°F = 120°C
275°F = 140°C
300°F = 150°C
325°F = 160°C
350°F = 180°C
375°F = 190°C
400°F = 200°C
425°F = 220°C
450°F = 230°C

BAKING PAN SIZES

Utensil	Size in Inches/Quarts	Metric Volume	Size in Centimeters
Baking or Cake Pan (square or rectangular)	8×8×2	2 L	20×20×5
	9×9×2	2.5 L	23×23×5
	12×8×2	3 L	30×20×5
	13×9×2	3.5 L	33×23×5
Loaf Pan	8×4×3	1.5 L	20×10×7
	9×5×3	2 L	23×13×7
Round Layer Cake Pan	8×1½	1.2 L	20×4
	9×1½	1.5 L	23×4
Pie Plate	8×1¼	750 mL	20×3
	9×1¼	1 L	23×3
Baking Dish or Casserole	1 quart	1 L	—
	1½ quart	1.5 L	—
	2 quart	2 L	—